D1608378

MORE FESTIVALS IN ASIA

Asian Copublication Programme Series Two
Sponsored by the Asian Cultural Centre for Unesco

MORE

KODANSHA INTERNATIONAL LTD.

Tokyo, New York and San Francisco

FESTIVALS IN ASIA

This book is published under the Asian Copublication Programme carried out, in cooperation with Unesco, by the Asian Cultural Centre for Unesco/Tokyo Book Development Centre. The stories have been selected and edited by a five-country editorial board with the help of Unesco member states in Asia.

Distributed in the United States by Kodansha International/USA Ltd., through Harper & Row Publishers, Inc., 10 East 53rd Street, New York, New York 10022, and in Japan by Kodansha International Ltd., 2-12-21 Otowa, Bunkyo-ku, Tokyo 112.

Published by Kodansha International Ltd., 2-12-21 Otowa, Bunkyo-ku, Tokyo 112 and Kodansha International/USA Ltd., 10 East 53rd Street, New York, New York 10022 and 44 Montgomery Street, San Francisco, California 94104. Copyright © 1975 by the Asian Cultural Centre for Unesco/Tokyo Book Development Centre, 6 Fukuro-machi, Shinjuku-ku, Tokyo. All rights reserved. Printed in Japan.

LCC 75-34740
ISBN 0-87011-273-2
JBC 8039-785248-2361

First edition, 1975

CONTENTS

TO CHILDREN EVERYWHERE

This book introduces the young reader to festivals in nine Asian countries. A festival is an occasion to wear new clothes, decorate the house, sing hymns, let off fireworks, prepare special meals and exchange good wishes. It can have a religious meaning or it may be associated with a particular season; but be it in Sri Lanka or be it in Afghanistan, the festivals have much in common, for the joy of living and gratitude for nature's bounties are universal.

June

Korea

TAN-O DAY

Chul-su and Kap-sun live in the same village and have a very special day ahead of them. Today is the fifth day of the fifth month in Korea, which usually falls in our month of June, and every year on this day a big celebration is held. It is Tan-O Day, and Chul-su and Kap-sun will compete in the big annual events.

On this morning Chul-su is up earlier than usual. He runs to the nearby stream outside his house, takes off his shirt and washes his face with the cool water. "Summer is here," he says to himself, for the willow trees by the river are brighter and greener than usual. "Ah! How good this feels." In fact, Chul-su is so happy that even the morning chorus of the forest birds sounds merrier.

This is the day Chul-su has been waiting for. The eleven-year-old boy has been picked to represent his village in the wrestling match for boys that is held on Tan-O Day. Chul-su has been training for it every day and he feels sure that he can win the little calf which is the prize. The men have their own match too, where the prize is a cow. And to prove to himself how strong he is, Chul-su clenches his fist and flexes his muscles. They feel firm.

On the way to the school playground where the match will be held, Chul-su remembers one boy, Soe-tol from the next village, who will be hard to fight. Soe-tol is twelve years old and very tall

9

and strong, his friends have told him. "But I am faster with my hands," thinks Chul-su.

Chul-su has brought Grandfather along with him to watch the wrestling. He picks a good ringside seat for Grandfather and then looks for his friends. Today the playground is all decked out with red and white banners, and in the center, underneath a tent roof, is the ring marked off for the wrestlers. His friends spot him by the ring and the next minute they are all shouting, "Hurray for Chul-su! Win them all, Chul-su!"

How nice to have such fine friends! Soon the playground fills with people, and the cotton candy man, the cake-seller and the taffy man have all found good places beside the ring. The farmers' band strikes up a lively tune, and from the corner of his eye Chul-su spies the little prize calf.

The match is about to begin and Chul-su changes into his sports clothes and gets in the ring to face his first opponent. The boys size each other up and when the referee gives them the starting signal, a tap on the shoulder, they lunge toward each other and soon they are locked together. Each tries to make his opponent fall or touch the ground with his hand. Chul-su proves the stronger of the two and he trips his opponent, making him fall. The crowd claps for Chul-su, the winner.

Before noon Chul-su has won five matches against the neighboring villages. Grandfather lights his pipe and beams happily at the boy. "Well done!" he says. "Let's have some lunch before you fight Soe-tol. You will need some food."

Lunchtime came and went, but Chul-su's thoughts were centered on Soe-tol. When the farmers' band struck up another tune, Chul-su stepped into the ring to face Soe-tol.   11

Even the adults have gathered around to watch this exciting final contest between the two boys.

To win the little calf Chul-su has to win two out of three matches. But Soe-tol was too strong for him and although Chul-su tried hard he lost the first match. The boy was downcast. Grandfather, seeing Chul-su so disappointed, came over to the ring and whispered something in his ear.

When the second match began Chul-su fought much better. He used his hands, which moved much faster than Soe-tol's, and confused his opponent by slapping him on the legs. Left! Right! Left! Right! they flicked. The second match went easily to Chul-su. Now they were tied, one match each. More and more cheers went up from the crowd. Chul-su looked at his grandfather. The white-haired man stroked his beard and nodded as if to say, "You're doing all right, Chul-su. Keep it up!"

Just before the final round the little calf was brought trotting into the ring in front of the wrestlers to encourage them. Chul-su and Soe-tol eyed the calf and each other. This time when they started to wrestle their skills were evenly matched. Chul-su moved faster, but Soe-tol was stronger. On and on they battled until beads of perspiration ran down their necks and their faces became puffed and red. Then Chul-su, summoning all the strength in his body, lifted Soe-tol off the ground. At the same time he wrapped his leg around Soe-tol's and pushed him backward. And suddenly both boys lost their balance and fell. The crowd gasped! But Soe-tol fell first and his body lay on the ground underneath Chul-su. The match went to Chul-su.

13

"Hurray for Chul-su! Hurray for our village! Our village is the best!" Screams and cheers broke out throughout the playground.

Grandfather looked at Chul-su with pride as the boy mounted the brown calf to ride around the village, as the winner usually does. And everybody cheered and clapped wherever he passed, saying, "Such a fine boy! Such fighting spirit! Well done, Chul-su! Well done!"

A little distance away from the wrestling match, in the village park, is a tall swing decorated with red and white strips of paper. This is for the girls' swing contest, which has been held on Tan-O Day for one thousand years. Each year on Buddha's birthday, a month before Tan-O Day, the gaily decorated swing is set up in the park and all the young girls in the village come to practice on it every day.

The girl who swings the highest will win a brand new sewing machine, the first prize. And to measure how high she swings a little bell is attached to a pole beside the swing. The girl who rings the bell most often will win the new sewing machine.

Most of the other girls in the village have already had their turn at the swing and now it is Kap-sun's turn. She has been practicing on the swing very hard, and as she walks toward it, she looks pretty in her blue silk blouse and pink skirt. These are the new clothes that she was finishing all day yesterday, for little Kap-sun is very fond of sewing, and hopes she can swing high enough to win the sewing machine. Her mother will be so pleased!

She remembers what her mother said just before she left the house in the morning. "Kap-sun, try and swing as high as you can." "Yes, Mother," she replied. "Come and watch me. I think I can win this year." Her mother promised that she would be at the park a little later.

As Kap-sun walked to the swing she suddenly heard a voice cry out from the crowd, "Do your best, Kap-sun! You can win!" It was her mother. And feeling all the strength enter her body Kap-sun got on the swing and pushed with all her might. Up and up the swing flew. Higher and higher it went with Kap-sun, like a pink and blue butterfly, flying into the sky. And each time she swung up she kicked the little bell with her foot. Ting! Ting! Ting! it rang, over and over again.

And very soon there was no doubt who had won the contest, for the little bell didn't stop ringing for a long time. The people in the crowd cheered the little girl's deter-

15

mination to win. "Such strength! Such spirit!" they murmured among themselves. "Well done, Kap-sun! I'm so proud of you!" her mother said when she got off the swing.

That evening her mother invited many people in the village to dinner at her house. She was so pleased that Kap-sun had won. And when the guests arrived the first thing they saw when they entered the room was the new sewing machine right in the middle of the table.

EID-UL-FITR

The ninth month of the Muslim calendar is known as Ramadan, the holy month. And throughout this month all Muslims make the good resolution not to eat or drink anything while the sun is in the sky. This is called fasting.

The thirty days of Ramadan pass slowly, and toward the end of the month everyone looks forward to the last day of the fast when they can celebrate the joyous festival of thanksgiving, which is called Eid-ul-Fitr in Pakistan. On that evening everyone will be out in the streets looking for the moon, for only when the moon is in the sky can they really know that the month of fasting has come to an end.

People climb up onto rooftops. Children stand on walls and porches. Thousands of eyes are fixed on the darkening sky. Is the moon up?

"I see it! I see it!" a child cries suddenly.

"Where? Where is it?" another child asks.

"I can't see it. Don't tease!" says a third.

An old lady hears the excitement outside and hurries onto her porch. She peers into the sky.

"The moon is up. Quick! Quick! Look at it before it disappears behind the clouds again," she tells the children.

17

"Oh, yes, I see the moon! I see the moon!" exclaims a little girl, jumping up and down with joy, her thick braids swinging about her face.

Then the streets echo with the cries and shouts of people, clamoring excitedly, "Look at the new moon! Look how clear and lovely it is!"

The last wisp of cloud drifts away and the new moon slips into view, a beautiful crescent of silver, the symbol of the Muslim faith. A sudden crackle of fireworks is heard from a nearby shop and the streets throb with excitement. There is so much to be done now that the fast is over. People hurry in all directions to make the last-minute preparations for the festival.

Girls dream of the sparkling glass bangles they will wear around their wrists for Eid. They will need new shoes and, of course, some henna dye to trace pretty red patterns on the palms of their hands, as they always do when there is a festival. Boys will need new suits and new prayer caps. Mothers will need to buy food and sweets for the thankgiving festival. And everybody will need new clothes to wear the next morning for this joyous festival.

So the hustle and bustle in the streets begins with people pushing and jostling, laughing and joking. Some spread prayer mats on the ground to pray. Many rush to the bazaar. And what a spread greets their arrival. There are fruit and betelnuts and sweets. There are brilliant glass bangles and pretty shoes. What crowds, what throngs, what happy spending! Mothers buy special vermicelli which they will cook golden-brown the next morning and serve with chopped almonds, pistachios, and grated coconut. And over the top they will place a paper-thin layer of silver, the special decoration for food eaten during festivals.

And right into the night the streets remain filled with people. "Buy what you need tonight! Buy what you wish tonight!" the vendors call. Indeed this is the night to buy, for the next day no shops will be open.

On the morning of Eid the mood is completely different. Everyone is up bright and early, and the men and boys put on new clothes and prayer caps to go to the mosque. The women and the girls will get everything ready in the house for the festival before they return.

The mosque soon fills with people who have come to say the Eid prayers. First the inner courtyard, then the outer courtyard, then the garden, the steps and even the streets leading to the mosque are full of men and boys. Some of them bring prayer mats with them. They all wait for the priest to signal the beginning of prayers.

Before this everyone has made the thanksgiving offer of money to the poor and needy. And when the priest calls out, "God is great! God is great!"

all hands are raised toward the sky, bodies bent forward and foreheads pressed against the ground in a gesture of praising the Lord.

After prayers are said, everyone rises. Those on the streets, those on the steps, those in the garden, those in the courtyard and those in the mosque. And as they rise they embrace and bless each other with the words "Eid Mubarak!" And their happy wishes are heard over and over again as they make their way home.

The women and girls await the men at home, and as soon as they return the houses echo with these greetings. The girls are dressed in the bright clothes bought at the bazaar the night before and the women look like birds of paradise in so many vivid colors. Glass bangles tinkle on their arms and sequins sparkle on their shoes as they sing out "Eid Mubarak" to one and all.

Silver coins are given by parents to their children, and near ones, far ones, old ones, dear ones meet again on this great day of thanksgiving.

21

By evening the children are ready for the different shows and games held at the fairground. Acrobats twist their bodies to perform skillful feats; jugglers toss plates in the air and catch them before they fall to the ground. The little girls and boys climb on horses to be whirled merrily about, and the bigger and braver ones rush to the ferris wheel to be spun up into the sky and down again.

At the fairground parrots perform pretty tricks to amuse the children. Monkeys dance, camels dance and even horses dance standing on their hind legs. Indeed, everything and everyone dances on this joyous occasion as Eid comes to Pakistan again.

September

Indonesia

LEBARAN

The boys are going to school without their schoolbags. Instead they bring marbles, tops and yoyos. Arman, Sidi, Yaman and I have brought our new football. It took us four months to save up our pocket money and buy it.

Today we have no lessons because it is the last day before Ramadan, when we have no school and everybody fasts for a whole month. We are gathered in the hall and our headmaster tells us to be good and obedient at home, to pray five times a day, to recite the Holy Book, and to visit the mosque every evening during Ramadan.

Soon we are on our way home. Arman, Sidi, Yaman and I are bouncing and kicking the ball. "Who wants to play soccer?" I ask. "I do! And I! Me, too!" they reply.

When we reached an empty field we divided into two teams with Arman and Sidi as captains and we played soccer in the sunshine. Many times I kicked the ball toward the goal, but Yaman, who was goalkeeper, was too quick for me. When his team cheered for him, I felt disappointed. Once I managed to get the ball into his penalty area, but Yaman ran up from behind and pulled me by my pants. The button snapped off and the boys laughed at me. I felt silly and annoyed.

"That's a foul!" I shouted angrily, pointing at Yaman, but nobody paid any attention. I got even angrier and waited for a chance to get even. So, when Yaman jumped up to catch a ball, I kicked him as hard as I could. Yaman fell.

"Foul! Foul! Free kick!" his team shouted.

"No! Yaman pulled me before!" I shouted back.

Yaman's leg was bleeding, but we continued to play until it was time to go home.

Mother was in the kitchen making something that smelt good for our dawn meal. During Ramadan we have to eat before the sun rises because while the sun is up we are not allowed to eat or drink. Father came home from work with good news. "Before the end of Ramadan I will take you to visit Granddad in the country. There we will celebrate the Lebaran festival, which comes after the month of the fast, when God has forgiven us our sins."

"Hurray!" I shout, even though Lebaran is a month away.

The next morning the ring of the alarm wakes me up. It is two o'clock and time for our dawn meal. After washing my face and brushing my teeth, I join my family around the dining table. There is fish, soup and rice that Mother has prepared.

Father asks me if I know the meaning of this meal. I shake my head.

24

"This meal, my son, is a gift from God, so be thankful to God for it and obey Him always," says Father seriously. Yes, the meal given by God is very tasty indeed.

"What shall I do today while I am fasting?" I wonder. I want to play soccer, but if I go to see Arman and Sidi I have to pass Yaman's house. To tell you the truth, I am afraid of what Yaman might do if he sees me. So all day long I sit around the house until the sun goes down and it is time for dinner. We prayed first and then had our dinner.

After dinner Father took me with him to the mosque. I saw Arman and Sidi there, but where was Yaman? Then I saw him sitting in the corner, but when he saw me, he looked away. Oh, how angry Yaman must be with me!

We prayed and recited the Holy Book and then we had some fruit. When it was time to leave, Yaman went out without saying a single word to me. And day after day, for nearly a whole month, Yaman did not speak to me.

One day, while I was fasting, Father asked me if I felt hungry. "Yes, Father, I am very hungry," I replied. "So remember, son, what it is like for the poor to be always hungry. That's why we try to help the poor by giving them food and money just before the Lebaran festival."

Three days before Lebaran Father showed us the train tickets he had bought. "Oh! we're going by train to visit Granddad!" I exclaimed. When we got to the station the day before Lebaran there was such a large crowd there. The capital city of Jakarta was empty because so many people were going to the country. The stationmaster blew his whistle and the train pulled out of the station.

At Granddad's house the gates and fences were all decorated with lamps for Lebaran. Uncles, aunts and little cousins came to the door and embraced us. Every room in the house was brightly lit with lamps. In the evening the big drum of the mosque sounded, followed by the chanting, "God is great!" We joined in the chanting and even on the streets we heard men and children saying "God is great! God is great!"

At the mosque Father offered a sack of rice and some money to the poor. Grandma, Mother and my aunts were at home cooking the *ketupat* rice, which we eat for our Lebaran meal.

The next day was Lebaran. We all put on our best clothes and went to a field for special prayers. The field was full of people lined up in long rows chanting "God is great!" After the prayers we greeted one another and asked for forgiveness. When we got home we ate the delicious Lebaran meal and then we all exchanged greetings and asked for forgiveness for our faults.

After spending five days with Granddad we left by train again for Jakarta. I was so tired after the trip that I fell asleep as soon as I got home.

Suddenly there is a knock at the door. Who can this be? Arman? Sidi? I open the door. It is Yaman! He greets me and I greet him. Then we hug each other. "Please forgive me," says Yaman. "And forgive me, too," I say.

I invite Yaman into the house for some mangoes. While we are eating there is another knock at the door. "Who's there?" I ask. It is Arman and Sidi. We exchange greetings and then we all sit down and eat mangoes together.

HARI RAYA PUASA

It was the twenty-sixth day of Ramadan and Azman and Aini were busy all afternoon making little lamps out of bamboo and tin cans and placing them just outside the house and in the garden. Now there was nothing more to do but wait until they could break their fast and light those lamps.

"Let's light them now," said Aini, the little girl.

"No, Aini," Azman replied. "We must wait until we hear the drum from the mosque first. It won't be long now."

Just then their mother Mak Esah called them from the house and the two children ran to the dining room to join their parents who were sitting around the table. And as soon as they heard the "Boom! Boom! Boom!" from the mosque echo through the village, all four raised a glass of water and drank it. Then they ate all the delicious food that Mak Esah had prepared. Their fast was over for the day.

"Aini, come, let's go and light the lamps," said Azman, beckoning her to follow him. And while Aini stood by and watched, Azman lit all the lamps around the house and in the garden. Soon little orange flecks of light danced around the house and in the garden and everything looked cheerful and lovely. If only they had more lamps, how beautiful their garden would be!

29

"Azman, let's make some more lamps for Hari Raya Eve," suggested Aini.

"That's a good idea, Aini," replied Azman. "Hari Raya is four days away and we will have time to collect more tin cans and bamboo."

Hari Raya is the first day of the tenth month of the Muslim calendar, known as Shawal, and the first day of Shawal is a national holiday for non-Muslims, and a religious holiday for all the Muslim people in Malaysia.

Their father, Pak Jamil, watched them from the veranda. As Azman and Aini walked back to the house, he smiled and put his hand in his bulging pocket.

"I have a surprise for you," he said, and brought out a handful of firecrackers and sparklers.

"Oh, thank you, Daddy!" exclaimed the children.

"Firecrackers, firecrackers," Azman shouted as he ran into the garden.

"Sparklers, sparklers," cried Aini, skipping happily behind her brother.

Then the two children joined their friends from next door, who were also lighting firecrackers. They continued to play until their father had returned from the mosque after prayers and it was time to go to bed.

By Hari Raya Eve the children had made twelve more lamps for the garden. They helped Mak Esah sweep the floors, dust the furniture and even paint all the flowerpots in the garden white. In the afternoon Pak Jamil took the children to the beach to collect young coconut leaves to wrap up the special rice, called *ketupat*, that is eaten on Hari Raya Day.

"I'll go and make the beef *rendang*," said Mak Esah with a smile, knowing how much Azman and Aini loved this food.

"Daddy, can we have some more fireworks for tonight?" asked Azman and Aini.

Pak Jamil promised he would give them some more, and before they went to bed that evening they had such a good time with their friends, lighting fireworks and letting off firecrackers until the whole village echoed with the noise.

Inside the house Mak Esah was hanging up new drapes on the windows and doors. She spread a new tablecloth over the table and put new covers on all the cushions. Everything was now neat and tidy for Hari Raya Day tomorrow.

That night both children were so excited that they could hardly fall asleep. They lay in their beds and dreamed of the delicious food they would eat and all their friends who would come to visit them on Hari Raya Day.

32 When they opened their eyes again it was day. Hari

Raya Day! The children rushed out of bed and into the bath. They scrubbed themselves properly because it was Hari Raya Day and there would be new clothes to wear.

Mak Esah had made a lovely pink sarong for Aini and some yellow trousers for Azman. Azman put on his new velvet cap and the new shoes that his father had bought him. Aini, too, had new red shoes to wear. When their parents had put on their new clothes, the family was ready to go out.

But before they left Mak Esah sat down in front of Pak Jamil to ask for his forgiveness. Everyone in Malaysia starts the new month by promising each other to be good and by forgiving each other for their bad deeds of the past. After Pak Jamil had forgiven Mak Esah he also took his wife's hand in his and asked to be forgiven. Now it was the children's turn to ask for forgiveness from their parents for being naughty or disobedient. And Pak Jamil and Mak Esah gladly forgave them.

Then the family set off to visit the cemetery of their relatives and to recite a passage from the Holy Book to those who were no longer with them to celebrate this festival. Mak Esah then took Aini home to prepare the meal while Pak Jamil and Azman went to the mosque to pray. After the Hari Raya prayers at the mosque they embraced all their friends and greeted them with the words, "Happy Hari Raya!"

A short while after Pak Jamil and Azman returned home the house was filled with friends and relatives who came to wish them Happy Hari Raya. And Azman and Aini's Chinese friends came, too, to wish them a happy holiday.

Mak Esah went into the kitchen to get food and drink and soon everyone was 33 enjoying the delicious beef *rendang* with *ketupat* rice. After the food they had cakes. "How good this tastes!" said Aini. And when they had eaten the children were eager to go out. "Where shall we go?" asked Aini. "Let's go to the movies in town," said Azman. "Then we can go and wish our friends there a Happy Hari Raya Day, too."

September

Vietnam

MID-AUTUMN FESTIVAL

Don't you think the night is beautiful when there's a full moon in the sky? We watch the moon closely in my country, Vietnam. A long time ago we made a calendar based on the movements of the moon, as did the people of Singapore and Korea. We think the full moon of the eighth month is especially lovely, and to celebrate its beauty, we hold the Mid-autumn Festival, which usually falls in your month of September. I think the best part of this festival is the special cake we eat, *banh trung-thu*, as round as the full moon itself and filled with delicious nuts and fruits. Everyone loves these mooncakes so much that sometimes there is almost no sugar left in the country at this time because so many people make mooncakes.

In olden days grownups celebrated the event by gathering on the porch at night to look at the moon, eating mooncakes and sipping tea. Sometimes they composed poems in honor of the moon, which covers the whole countryside with a silvery tinge. But now we children have the most fun as this festival is also celebrated as Children's Day. We walk around the streets with our lighted lanterns and there is so much dancing and rejoicing that by midnight everyone is tired and ready for bed.

Most of the lighted lanterns we carry around are simple round

ones, shaped like the full moon, but this year I have a lantern that is shaped like a fish. Our grandparents make the lanterns for us and sometimes they make beautiful ones that move. Well, actually, a ring of cardboard figures inside the lantern turns around slowly when the candles in the lantern are lit. The figures inside tell stories from old legends and fairy tales. When the heat of the candles makes the figures turn, you can see them revolving slowly against the thin paper of the lantern.

On the day of the festival my mother tries to make the very best mooncakes. The other women and girls in the village try, too. There is a mooncake contest each year in the evening and we children all come, bringing the light of our little lanterns. The cakes are put on show for all to see, and if a girl can make tasty mooncakes, she will have no trouble finding a husband. But we are not allowed to eat the mooncakes until later on in the evening. You see, our mothers place the paper figure of an ancient doctor, no one knows exactly why, in the middle of each tray of cakes, and until the paper doctor is removed, we are not allowed to touch them.

After the mooncake contest we all wait for the dancing dragons to come down the street. There are two sorts of dragon dances, one done by grownups and one by children. Musicians march in the streets beating huge drums, clashing cymbals and carrying banners. And when the drums beat louder and louder and the cymbals clash more and more noisily, you know that the dance is about to begin.

The dancers underneath the dragon move about in a zigzag fashion, those at the front carry the dragon's head while those at the end carry its tail. Quite a few dragons come up, twisting and twirling around, writhing like snakes and dancing to the rhythm of the big drums. The dancers go from street to street, and wherever they appear, children rush out of their houses with their lighted lanterns to watch. What an exciting parade!

Often there is a contest to decide which is the best dancing dragon and the winning group celebrates by letting off hundreds of little red firecrackers. And then there is so much noise and so much shouting that you can't hear the drums anymore.

In some villages in Vietnam there is a songfest performed by local girls and boys. They gather in the middle of a field and if it is held at night the spectators carry lighted lanterns. In the middle of the singers a large pot is turned upside down and a rope is stretched over the top of the pot. The ends of the rope are tied to stakes that are driven into the ground. The girls and boys take their places at opposite sides of the rope and sing.

Usually they start with their favorite Vietnamese folksongs and while they sing they beat the taut rope with bamboo sticks. The sounds the rope makes when hit with the sticks are like the notes of a musical instrument. As they continue, the boys and girls make up new lines of their own for the songs to tease and challenge one another while the onlookers clap and cheer at the end of each song. Both the singers and the spectators have such a wonderful time that it is difficult for them to stop.

A lot of romances begin during the Mid-autumn Festival as the singers fall in love with each other on this special evening. And eventually they even get married and have

children, and when their children grow up they also take part in these songfests, just as their parents did a long time ago. But for the younger children it is the mooncakes, the colored lanterns and the dragon dances that they will remember most clearly for weeks and weeks after.

October

Nepal

DASAIN

In the distant kingdom of Nepal, tucked away in the Himalaya Mountains, the biggest festival, Dasain, comes in the cool, clear month of October. Dasain is a religious celebration that goes on for ten days, and like Christmas, there is a wonderful story behind it.

A long, long time ago, the story goes, two powerful demons, Madhu and Kaitava, ruled the earth. So wicked was their rule that the lives of the people were filled with fear and dread, but no one could lift a little finger against the terrible pair. One day Durga, goddess of power, took pity on the people, and disguised as Kali, goddess of war, challenged the demons to a duel. The demons fought as hard as they could, but they were no match for the goddess. When Durga killed them, peace and order returned to earth and the people rejoiced that they were no longer in the grip of the wicked demons. And for ten days after Durga's victory they ate, drank and gave thanks to Durga for ridding the earth of the tyrants. And even to this day the people of Nepal eat, drink, make merry, say prayers, put on their best clothes and offer sacrifices to Durga. Let's join the merrymakers in Kathmandu and see what happens there during Dasain.

The people make all their preparations for the festival in 41

advance and then wait for the day to arrive, just like we do at Christmas. A week before, the houses are swept and everything inside washed and cleaned. In Kathmandu the doors are even painted a bright red during this time.

The shopkeepers, knowing that people will need to buy new clothes, caps and shoes for Dasain, compete with one another in arranging the most attractive displays. All the new goods that they have saved up for the festival are brought out and hung up, and windows are specially shined to make the goods stand out more clearly. The twisting lanes of Kathmandu are filled with mothers, fathers and children busily hunting for good bargains.

✦   ✦   ✦

On the first day of Dasain every member of the family is up bright and early for the special ceremony that begins the festival. This takes place in the prayer room of each house. A jar of water is placed on a stand that is covered with a layer of dung. Beside the jar of water a handful of river sand is placed and in it a few barley seeds are planted and then watered. Prayers are said in front of the jar of water, which is said to be the symbol of Durga's power.

✦   ✦   ✦

On the second day of Dasain right up to the sixth day prayers are said in front of the jar every morning. The day is taken up with visits to the temples to pray to Durga. The inside of the temple is amazingly transformed during this time, filled with flowers, fragrant incense and flickering candles. It is as though Durga herself is present in the midst of the people who are praying to her. Everyone is dressed in their very best and they walk from temple to temple with light hearts, happy to honor the kind and generous Durga.

◆   ◆   ◆

On the seventh day of Dasain Kathmandu becomes even more colorful. This is the day when an offering of flowers is carried from one end of the city to the other. This Fulpati procession is accompanied by music from a military band and a special gun salute at the end of the procession. Hearts flutter at the roar of the guns and at the sight of the king and queen of Nepal, who come to join the prayers at Hanumandhoka Temple. The streets of Kathmandu are crowded with visitors from neighboring towns and villages who come to see the Fulpati procession and to catch a glimpse of their beloved king and queen.

◆   ◆   ◆

On the eighth day of Dasain the goddess is worshipped in a different way. This is the day when millions of goats, buffaloes and

44

fowls are sacrificed in all homes and temples in Kathmandu in honor of Durga. It is a joyous day ending with the biggest and most magnificent banquet of the year.

✦   ✦   ✦

On the ninth day of Dasain no cars, motorcycles, buses or machines of any kind will move in the city. This is the day when the sacrifices of the eighth day are repeated, not for Durga herself, but for the power that makes cars and machines work. The people of Nepal believe that it is the goddess Durga who gives all machines the power of movement, and thus everything is kept still and silent on that day.

✦   ✦   ✦

On the tenth day of Dasain everything moves! How different are the festivities! This day commemorates Rama's victory over the demon king a long time ago—with the help of Durga, naturally! Children ask for blessings from their parents, grandparents, aunts and uncles. They receive a red dot

45

of paste called *tika* on their foreheads and a new shoot of barley is put on their heads with the words, "May the goddess grant you all your wishes and help you against evil!" And soon in the streets of Kathmandu you will see children and grownups alike walking around with lots of red *tika* on their foreheads and barley shoots peeping out from under their caps. They are on their way to the homes of friends and relatives to ask for more blessings. Everyone is happy and content, for they know that they have the protection of Durga in the coming year and they look forward to the next day with eagerness.

In the evening a last act of thanks is paid to Durga with a procession where people carry precious weapons of ancient times in the streets of Kathmandu. But in some regions of Nepal the last tribute to Durga takes the form of a sword dance, a fitting replay of Durga's "dance" with the demon kings of long ago.

DIWALI
FESTIVAL OF LIGHTS

Ten-year-old Dipa shook her little brother's shoulder. "Wake up, Chandu! Wake up!"

For the past week Dipa has been getting up very early in the morning to help Mother and Grandmother with the housecleaning for Diwali, the biggest and brightest festival in India. At this time of year, October to November, all homes in India, whether a small hut or a rich mansion, are whitewashed and painted. Dipa knows that if the house is not spick and span, Lakshmi, the goddess of good luck and prosperity, will not visit them that year. So Dipa helped Mother wash all the floors, polish all the furniture, and scrub all the kitchen pots until they gleamed like new. And two days before the festival Grandmother went to the market and returned with two shining new cooking pots, just as everyone does for Diwali.

"Wake up! Chandu!" Dipa called once more.

Chandu stirred and rubbed his sleepy eyes.

"Have you forgotten what day it is today? It's Diwali! And we have so much to do. Hurry and get dressed, Chandu. You know that Grandmother says we should rise with the sun on Diwali because Goddess Lakshmi doesn't like lazy people."

With that Dipa skipped off again to help Mother. Now they

47

were both going to decorate the living room floor with *rangoli*. Mother was very clever at drawing pretty pictures of birds and flowers on the floor with white rice powder and Dipa's favorite task was to fill in the drawings with red, blue, pink and yellow powder. When she had finished coloring, Dipa's mother looked very pleased. The room really did look bright and cheerful. She then went to the entrance and drew one last pattern on the floor as a sign of welcome to the visitors who would be coming to see them on Diwali.

"Dipa, tell Chandu to come and help us with the candy boxes," said Mother with a smile.

Dipa ran off to fetch Chandu. She knew that Chandu loved to make candy boxes as much as she did. Each year Mother would get many little boxes ready, and Dipa and Chandu would then fill them up with the delicious sweets Mother and Grandmother had made. They had to take one candy box to each of the uncles, aunts and friends they visited that afternoon. And best of all, they would also receive a candy box from each visitor to their house. What a lovely day Diwali is!

When the candy boxes had been filled, Dipa and Chandu had their own task to do. The

night before, Father had taken them to the
bazaar and bought two hundred little *diwa*
lamps, and Dipa and Chandu had to place them
all over the house. These lamps are made of clay
specially for the festival and sold in all the
bazaars a few days before. And when evening
came and the lamps were lit the house would
look as fabulous as a palace!

There is an old story behind these *diwa* lamps.

✦   ✦   ✦

A very long, long time ago in the rich and flourishing city of Ayodhya in India,
there lived a good king called Dasrath. As the king was getting very old he wanted to
make his son, Rama, the next king of Ayodhya. But the king had a second wife, Rama's
stepmother, who wanted to put her own son on the throne. As she had once saved the
king's life, he promised to grant her one wish, whatever she desired. So she asked the old
king to banish Rama to the forest for fourteen years so that her son could sit on the
throne. The old king was heartbroken, but he could not break his promise.

So Rama was sent into the forest together with his wife, Sita, and his brother
Lakshmana. Together they built a hut to live in and Rama and Lakshmana hunted in
the forest for food. One day they were visited by the demon princess Surpankha, who

fell in love with Rama and wanted to marry him. When Lakshmana heard this he was so furious with Surpankha that he drew his sword and cut off her nose. Surpankha was very offended and swore that she would get her revenge.

Now Surpankha had a brother who was the powerful demon king of Lanka, and he had magic powers. The demon king thought of a plan. He turned one of his uncles into a golden deer and sent him to graze by the forest hut of Rama and Sita. When Sita saw the golden deer she wanted very much to keep it as a pet and asked Rama and Lakshmana to catch it for her.

While the brothers were in the forest chasing the golden deer, the demon king, disguised as a holy man, came up to the hut to beg for alms. Sita could not refuse the holy man, so she opened the door. No sooner had she done this than the demon king threw off his disguise and carried her off in his flying chariot to Lanka.

Rama and Lakshmana heard what had happened and set off to rescue Sita. Month after month they searched for Lanka, and on their travels they befriended the Monkey King, Hanuman, who had an army of clever monkeys. And with

Hanuman's help the brothers found the city of Lanka and after a ten-day-long battle killed the demon king and brought Sita back.

The fourteen years of exile were now over and Rama could return to Ayodhya to rule as king. When the people of Ayodhya heard that Rama was coming back, they were so delighted that they lit lamps throughout the city to welcome him. And when Rama reached Ayodhya that evening, the city was bathed in light and the people rejoiced and made merry until dawn, for their beloved king had returned.

And so, ever since, Diwali, the festival of lights, is celebrated in memory of Rama, who destroyed the forces of evil and who is, himself, a symbol of all that is good and noble and virtuous.

✦   ✦   ✦

Chandu and Dipa got dressed in their new clothes to visit friends and relatives in the afternoon. Chandu had on his purple shirt and an embroidered waistcoat over it, and new trousers. Dipa chose her long skirt with bands of red and blue all over. They loaded both arms with candy boxes and set off with Mother and Father.

When they got home just before nightfall the two children joined their parents and their grandmother in the living room for prayers to Goddess Lakshmi for good luck and prosperity in the coming year. They put a garland of flowers around her statue and lit many sticks of incense which made the room smell sweet and fresh. And when the prayers were said, Grandmother blessed them both and pressed a spot of red paste on their foreheads. Their parents blessed them, too, and gave them money for toys.

Then the children went out to spend their gift money. The streets were full of gaily decorated shops, for Diwali marks the beginning of a new year for all shopkeepers. And the bazaar was full of people who were admiring the toys, fireworks, sweets and fruit. Dipa and Chandu bought some mud toys and some fireworks.

Very soon it was time to light the *diwa* lamps. How beautiful the house looked with two hundred flickering lights glowing in the dark. Now their parents took them to the main square to see the lights in the city. On the way they passed streets that were lined

with little booths. When Dipa and Chandu got to the square they could hardly believe how bright the city looked with colored lights everywhere. Look at those blue stars revolving around the yellow circles of light on that building! Look at those red lights over there! And the green ones! This must be what Ayodhya looked like when Rama returned!

When it was late and Chandu was too tired to walk, the family came home. Father had one last surprise for them on the roof. For right in the middle of the flat roof there

was a huge paper balloon with a candle in it. When Father lit the candle the balloon slowly puffed up with air and started to rise. Higher and higher it went, over the rooftops and into the sky. Dipa and Chandu clapped their hands.

"Where will it go?" Dipa wondered as she gazed at the balloon. "Please fly around the world to wish Happy Diwali to children everywhere," she wished aloud.

November

Thailand

LOY KRATHONG

My name is Ging and I am a girl of twelve. I live in Bangkok, the capital of Thailand, with my parents and my brother Garn, who is ten. Today Garn and I have come home with very little homework to do. Our teachers know we won't have much time since it is Loy Krathong Day.

Loy Krathong is my favorite festival. It takes place on the full moon night of the twelfth lunar month, which generally falls in the second half of November. *Loy* means "to float," and *krathong* "leaf cups." So this is the festival of floating leaf cups with lighted candles in them on rivers and canals.

Garn's favorite festival is Songkran, the water festival, which is gay and a lot of fun. But I prefer Loy Krathong because it is so much gentler and prettier, with the beautiful moon in the sky and hundreds of lights in the water.

You may wonder what the meaning of Loy Krathong is. To tell the truth, we are not very sure ourselves why we celebrate it. Some people believe that it is to ask the pardon of the goddess of the water for having made the rivers and canals dirty throughout the year. Others say that it is an act of worshiping Buddha's footprint, which he left on the shores of the Nammada river. But one thing we do know is that it is an old festival, six or seven hundred

55

years old, and it has been a joyful celebration for everyone for as long as that.

Anyhow, the origins aren't really important to me. The important thing is to have a nice *krathong* of my own. So here I am, sitting with my old nanny, with lots of banana leaves and other things needed for making *krathong*. My old nanny, who up to this year has always made a *krathong* for me, says that I must now make one myself. So I will try.

To make a *krathong* you have first to cut two round pieces out of a banana leaf. My hands are not very steady with a knife and I have wasted several leaves before cutting two perfect round pieces. With the two circles one on top of the other, I make a five-cornered cup, fastening each seam with a sharp bamboo pin.

I am quite pleased with my cup really, but Nanny takes one look at it, sighs, and says that it will never float properly since it is lopsided. So she gives in and makes me another cup, decorating the edges with strips of banana leaf sewn on with needle and cotton. She lets me stick jasmine and everlasting flowers along the edges, and then we stuff the center of the *krathong* with small pieces of banana trunk. We cover these with a piece of leaf, and in the middle we put incense sticks, one slim candle and three gardenias, which smell heavenly!

My *krathong* is now finished, but as we still have lots of banana leaves left over, Nanny says she will quickly make some simple cups for the cook to put steamed fish soufflé in. I want her to make some tiny square ones for the delicious nut pudding, but she says firmly that she has quite enough to do!

Now Garn comes bouncing in with an enormous *krathong* made of bright green tissue paper in the shape of a house. He has just bought it from the corner shop and is so pleased with it. But I am sure it will catch fire as soon as he lights the candles in it. As usual he's got a large supply of fireworks and some bangers which I hate. But, as Nanny says, boys will be boys, I suppose.

By and by our friends and relations come. As our house is on a canal, we invite our 57 cousins and friends to come and float their *krathong* with us. With so many guests tonight, dinner is filled with lively conversation.

After dinner we go out to our *sala*, the little wooden house built on the edge of the canal. The table in the *sala* is covered with *krathong* of all shapes and sizes. I see some traditional *krathong* like my own, but many people, like Garn, want to be different. Nid, my friend from across the street, has a beautiful white lotus made of lily leaves. Garn's best friend has carved a barge out of a banana tree and decorated it with flags and tassels. But the sweetest one of all is a simple boat made from a piece of coconut husk belonging to Oy, our cook's two-year-old daughter. She can hardly talk yet, but she knows the Loy Krathong song: "Loy, loy krathong! Loy, loy krathong! Let's all come, loy krathong. . . ."

While we all join Oy in the singing, the moon has risen in the clear, cloudless sky. Now it is time to float our *krathong*. Garn runs to the bank and sets his on the water. I make a wish as I carefully set mine on the water. May dear Aunt Charu, who has been studying in Europe for over a year, come home soon! It is said that if the light in your *krathong* lasts until the *krathong* disappears, your wish will come true. So I keep my eyes on my *krathong*, which drifts further and further, its little light still shimmering, until it disappears from view. "Oh! My wish will come true! Aunt Charu will come home soon!"

While I am still dreaming of Aunt Charu, a sudden "Bang, bang," startles me. Garn and his friends have started the fireworks. We are lucky this year to have a lot of "falling

rain," a special kind of firework which comes in earthenware pots from Chiengmai, our northern capital. When all the fireworks are lit at once the whole garden looks like a fairyland. But soon the boys' supply runs out and the place becomes dark and peaceful again.

The moon is now high, just over the pointed roof of our *sala*, which casts a beautiful silhouette on the lawn. The water on the canal looks silvery, dotted with little flickering lights. Music is heard, faintly, from afar. I stand up and walk toward the house. I think I will write to Aunt Charu tonight to tell her all about Loy Krathong this year.

December

Afghanistan

THE BUZKASHI GAME

As the days begin to get slightly chilly, men and boys in Afghanistan become excited by the thought of the buzkashi games. No one will miss a single buzkashi game because buzkashi is as closely followed in Afghanistan as baseball is in the United States. Yet buzkashi is nothing like baseball or any other game you have seen because it is only played in Afghanistan, and on horseback!

When the fall season begins the once-empty field is filled with men and horses. Boys shove and push their way through the crowd to catch a glimpse of their favorite players, for every young boy in Afghanistan dreams of becoming a good buzkashi player when he grows up. In the center of the field are the men on horseback. What magnificent animals they have! What fine, gleaming pelts! What courageous horsemen in their warm, quilted jackets and sheepskin caps! The boys are both thrilled and amazed at the sight of their heroes.

"Where is the *buz*?" They look around the field, and once they see the starting point, they catch sight of the body of a calf that is called the *buz*. When the signal is given, all the riders will try and pick up the *buz* from the starting point and carry it back again. And with one hundred horsemen all trying to snatch the *buz* from each other, the competition becomes so tough that it can take a whole afternoon for the *buz* to be brought back to the starting point by the winner of the game.

The riders, with whips in their hands to prod their horses, are beginning to form a circle. The boys hold their breath while they wait for the starting signal. "Bang!" And with this the horsemen make a beeline for the *buz*, kicking up so much dust that for a moment the boys cannot see what is happening. As the dust begins to settle the boys catch sight of the riders pushing, jostling and elbowing one another to get nearer the *buz*, or to prevent others from getting to it.

In the midst of the fighting horsemen the boys suddenly spot their favorite player Murad, on a fine, white stallion. Murad is also trying to get as close to the *buz* as possible, and as he moves toward it, his stallion suddenly lowers its forelegs to allow Murad to pick up the *buz*. When this happens a cheer goes up from the boys. Now Murad is moving out of the circle of horsemen and galloping into the distance.

"Murad is the finest player in the country!" the boys exclaim, their eyes fixed on the figure in the distance, leading all the other horsemen who are trying their best to catch him up. And more cheers go up from the spectators who admire the excellent horsemanship Murad displays.

As Murad gallops away with the *buz*, he suddenly feels someone coming up close behind him. He turns around to see that it is Qurban, his old rival, gaining ground on his black horse. In the past three years Qurban has always lost the game to Murad, but this year he is determined to win. He must win! And he spurs his horse with a sharp

crack of the whip. So fiercely do these two riders compete that they leave the others far behind.

The crowds watch with bated breath. And suddenly they gasp. Ooooh! Murad has fallen off his horse. And then Qurban falls, and the crowds gasp again. But both men pick themselves up, get on their horses again and ride off as though nothing has happened. The race is close.

The spectators can still see the riders in the distance. The boys have to squint to tell who is leading. "Murad is winning! Murad is the best!" they say jumping with joy. And suddenly someone shouts, "Qurban is catching up! Qurban has the *buz*! Come on, Qurban!"

Indeed the two men are galloping side by side, each holding onto part of the *buz*. Qurban is pulling and riding as hard as he can, but still he cannot snatch the *buz* from Murad. As they ride on, their whips in their hands, shouting and hollering on top of their voices, the slope of the mountain slowly looms up. Ahead a river

64

flows down the mountain slope, its water tumbling down in torrents. The men have to think fast. Should they turn around before they both fall in and drown?

Murad begins to steer his horse around, but Qurban, with his hands on the *buz* does not let Murad turn. They continue to ride straight along until Murad notices the track getting narrower. The river lay right in their path. "Turn! Turn!" he shouts to Qurban. But too late. In a second both men have fallen in the river.

The boys lost sight of the riders and began to fear for their safety. The sun, too, was beginning to set behind the mountain slope and some of the men in the crowd were turning away to go home for dinner. A party of riders decided to go after Murad and Qurban to find out if anything had happened to them. "Had they fallen and hurt themselves?" the boys wondered.

After some time a shout echoed across the hills. "They're coming back! They're coming back!" And gradually the small figure of a rider appeared on the faraway horizon. "Someone's got the *buz*! Who is it? Who is it?" The boys grew more and more excited. And in an instant they cheered and clapped, recognizing the riding style of Murad, their favorite player. And very soon cheers and shouts filled the entire field as Murad galloped closer and closer to the starting point to put the *buz* down.

The boys made way for their hero when he dismounted. Tired and worn out, Murad hardly noticed the claps and cheers as he walked stiffly through the line of spectators. He sat down on a rock and loosened the collar of his jacket and took off his hat.

In the twilight people could see the whip lashes on his forehead and dried blood on 65

his face. And as he lifted his hand to his face they saw that his hands, too, were badly injured.

The villagers invited Murad to dance and sing in the evening, but Murad seemed too weary. He was sad and silent. He would remember Qurban for a long time.

ACKNOWLEDGMENTS

TAN-O DAY

Written by Deok-sun Chang
Translated by Genell Y. Poitras
Illustrated by Kwang-bae Kim

EID-UL-FITR

Contributed by Mehr Nigar Masroor
Illustrated by B.A. Najmee

LEBARAN

Written by Sugiarta
Illustrated by Mardian

HARI RAYA PUASA

Written by Othman Puteh
Translated by Yeop Johari Yaakub
Illustrated by Mohammad Hassan

MID-AUTUMN FESTIVAL

Written by Vo Phien, Doan The Nhon
Translated by Trinh Viet Thai
Illustrated by Nguyen Thi Hop

DASAIN

Written by Keshav Raj Aryal

DIWALI FESTIVAL OF LIGHTS

Written by Uma Anand
Illustrated by Sanat Surti

LOY KRATHONG

Written by Napa Bhongbhibhat
Illustrated by Manat Na Chiengmai

THE BUZKASHI GAME

Written by Mohammad Reshad Wasa
Translated by Abdul Haq Walah
Illustrated by Nabiwalah Kakar